Evangelical Christianity Is A Cult

Why I Left Evangelicalism

by
Adam Lee

CCB Publishing
British Columbia, Canada

Evangelical Christianity Is A Cult:
Why I Left Evangelicalism

Copyright ©2023 by Adam Lee
ISBN-13   978-1-77143-557-4
First Edition

Library and Archives Canada Cataloguing in Publication
Title: Evangelical Christianity is a cult : why I left evangelicalism / by Adam Lee.
Names: Lee, Adam, 1978- author.
Issued in print and electronic formats.
ISBN 9781771435574 (softcover) | ISBN 9781771435581 (PDF)
Additional cataloguing data available from Library and Archives Canada

All Scriptural quotes are from the 1987 version of the KJV Bible and are in the Public Domain.

Cover artwork credit: Confused Man is Lost in the Forest
© alphaspirit | CanStockPhoto.com

Disclaimer: SEE YOUR PHYSICIAN. The information in this book is not intended to replace that of your physician and does not constitute medical advice. Do not use this book in place of proper medical care. Readers are advised to seek professional medical assistance in the event that they are suffering from any medical problem. All health questions concerning yourself or anyone else, must initially be addressed by your doctor or physician.

Extreme care has been taken by the author to ensure that all information presented in this book is accurate and up to date at the time of publishing. Neither the author nor the publisher can be held responsible for any errors or omissions. Additionally, neither is any liability assumed for damages resulting from the use of the information contained herein.

All rights reserved. No part of this publication may be reproduced, stored in a retrieval system or transmitted in any form or by any means, electronic, mechanical, photocopying, recording or otherwise without the express written permission of the publisher.

Publisher: CCB Publishing
              British Columbia, Canada
              www.ccbpublishing.com

Contents

Introduction v

Chapter 1: The Beginning 1

Chapter 2: Twins 5

Chapter 3: Reconciled 23

Chapter 4: Changed or Not Changed 49

Chapter 5: Life After Divorce 61

Chapter 6: The Truth 65

Chapter 7: Church Mayhem 67

Chapter 8: Delusions 71

Chapter 9: Evangelical Christianity Is A Cult! 79

Chapter 10: So, I Left Evangelicalism 83

Contact the Author 89

Introduction

These days most Americans still identify as Christians. It is the majority here in the United States of America where our coins still say, "In God We Trust." But there is a trend going on where more and more people are not attending church or identifying as religious anymore. There is also a trend going on in which people are just plain leaving the faith and deconstructing. Throughout this book I mention Christianity being a cult. But what I am really referring to is a certain branch of Christianity, the one I have had all the experiences in. I am referring to Evangelicalism and Evangelical Christianity. I do not believe that all of Christianity is a cult at all. Just Evangelicalism. There are things that aren't good outside of Evangelicalism that are found in Christianity as a whole that I may not see as good. But I just want to make clear that in this book I am mainly referring to Evangelicalism as being the cult.

Chapter 1

The Beginning

Every story has a beginning and mine began when I was a child. I had been pretty much raised as a Christian. Went to Sunday school at a Methodist church in those early years and learned that "Jesus loves me this I know." Believing in God was something I never questioned, and I was taught to respect the Bible as well. My family did not live as sold-out Christians though. We swore, we watched the series Married with Children, we fought, and it was a rare occasion that we would ever pray over a meal. Yet God was part of our lives. I grew up as a wild child and got in trouble a lot, whether it was at school or at home someone was always needing to discipline me. I had fun though and enjoyed my childhood very much. In my preteen years my mother got more religious and really engrained herself into church. She had gone to some revival meetings in nearby town and caught the on fire for Jesus bug. What followed was her pulling my aunt and uncle as well as my father into an itinerant praise and worship band. My mom wrote a lot of the songs for the band and it turned out she was a pretty talented song writer.

As she got more involved in church, I also got more involved in Bible lessons although they didn't mean much to me. I learned the core things like Jesus died for my sins, salvation can only come through faith in Him and stories like Adam and Eve and Noah. I did not get deep into the Bible or spend a lot of time around other Christian kids my age though. I had my group of friends and for the most part we liked to raise a little hell. So, for the better part of my teen years, I did raise a lot of hell and had a lot of fun doing it. By my mid-teens there had been a falling out with my mom's worship band and her church she was head over heels with fell apart. The pastor turned out to be some womanizer charlatan and left the church he started. My mom and dad (but my dad was really not that into it) kind of walked away from churches and being on fire for God. My mom said she got turned off by all the stuff she went through, but she still loved God, was a Christian, and reverenced the Bible.

I had a lot of misfortunes that befallen me. Life led me down a path that tamed me down a bit and then when I was 21, I got married. Marriage wasn't easy and the truth is I married the first girl that came along. I had had a lot of girlfriends before, but it never lasted long and we didn't get that close. This one was different; I was in love or maybe it was just plain old lust. She was all wrong for me, but she had gotten pregnant, so I thought the right thing to do was to marry her. So, 9 months after we met, we were married and expecting our first child. I learned that raising a child and being married was not an easy thing. My wife had an anger problem and I had depression and anxiety issues. The depression and anxiety as it turned out were not due to circumstances or my marriage, they were part of an inherited disorder, but circumstances sure didn't help it any.

I was not happy, and I felt like life was headed down the wrong path. I had remembered people preaching to me in the past saying that asking Jesus to come into your heart and change you will make everything all better. I felt that something was missing in my life, and I knew things needed to change. So, I started to ask Jesus to come into my heart and change me. I prayed that way for what seemed like a couple of years, and nothing happened. Things just went on as usual. Then one night as I was praying that prayer yet again, I heard an almost audible voice while I was lying in bed next to my wife and it said, "The hands of the father shall pass, the sins shall rise, and the darkness shall lift." I was so excited! I was thinking, wow God just spoke to me. But I did not understand what he said, and it would be something I would ponder for the next couple of weeks. Then one day after Christmas my wife had taken a pregnancy test because she missed her period and it revealed she was pregnant. I was bewildered. We had been taking precautions when I was intimate with her how did she get pregnant? I voiced my concern to her, and she broke down crying. It took me a second, but it occurred to me this child may not be mine. I asked her if she had been cheating and through her tears and sobs, she shook her head yes. In the course of the next hour or so I learned she had had an affair with my best friend. It was obvious he was the father, and I was not. I confronted him and he admitted it and that was where our friendship ended.

I was not going to raise this child and was making plans to divorce her. And to tell you the truth I don't know anyone in my situation who would have. Then a week or so later a friend of my mom's asked my mom, and I to go to a church service at her church on New Year's Eve. There was going to be a special speaker there and I had nothing better to do so I went.

It was cold that Wisconsin winter, but the church seemed nice with warm welcomes. The service did not make much sense to me, but I managed to endure it. Towards the end the minister who was speaking was coming up to people in the crowd and praying over them. For some people he would have a word from God. He come over to the place I was sitting, and he said I pray that the darkness lifts. I was like say what? He had said the very thing God spoke to me. I was blown away but hooked. I wanted to know what that meant so I asked him afterward and he said he had no clue. I left that night with an awe of God. And awe of church and an awe for the supernatural.

Chapter 2

Twins

A couple of months later my wife had an ultrasound which revealed that she was not pregnant with just one child, but two. She was going to have twins! To tell you the truth, I laughed when I heard it was twins. I knew that the twins were most likely Jacob's (my best friend), and when I heard there would be more than one, I thought, "There is justice in the world. My ex-friend would be stuck with double the child support and she would have double the burden of raising two babies at once." I was sure God was punishing them. Little did I know that what looked like a punishment for them would actually turn out to affect me just as much.

Even though things didn't look good at this point, it seemed in the coming months that God had a plan. As all this was happening, I remembered what the Lord had told me that night while I was praying for God to come into my heart and change me once again. God said, "The hands of the father shall pass, the sins shall rise, and the darkness shall lift." The sins were rising to the surface, my wife's sin with my best friend was out of the closet, next God was going to help me to see clearly and lift the darkness from all areas of my life. This was just the beginning of our journey. It's sad that it took such hurting and trials to get our attention, but sometimes that is the only way. Though looking back now that journey took to me to a different place than originally planned.

Throughout that time, I continued to attend church. I may not have, except a young man named Brent who saw me at a local thrift store and recognized me from the revival meeting. He invited me to the church for a Sunday morning service. Just like the last time I was invited to church, I had nothing better to do so I accepted the invitation.

The first Sunday morning service I attended at the church was, to say the least, something different for me. Sunday service was at 9:30 AM, and I made extra sure that I woke early enough to go. It was about a 15-minute drive to church, but I made it in time and was actually a bit early. The first thing I noticed was that this church was packed. The building itself was small, but wow, there sure were a lot of people there. Some people had to sit in the foyer instead of finding room in a pew. They seemed nice, and Brent and his friends asked me to sit with them. I didn't mind being there until the music started. It must have gone on for forty minutes or so, and it was all about Jesus.

The music was contemporary (which I liked), but I just wasn't into all that singing about Jesus. As I looked around, I saw people doing all kinds of different things. About ten percent of the people lifted their hands to heaven and seemed to be having an emotional experience. The rest of the people in the church either stood and clapped along to the songs or just sat there frowning with their arms crossed. I think it was about half and half with the clapping and arms crossed thing. I wasn't sure what to do, so I just sat there and prayed for the music to end soon.

I later learned that this was normal for a charismatic Word of Faith Church. The worship was geared towards an emotional experience. I had not had an emotional anything yet, other than being emotionally hurt. Lifting my hands and crying out to God just wasn't my thing at this time, but that would soon change.

When the music stopped there was a time for greeting your neighbor, and then the message began. During the message I was able to get a good look at the pastor. Pastor Tom was a younger man in his forties who actually looked and talked like Ned Flanders from "The Simpsons" TV show. Ned Flanders was the Christian goody two-shoes neighbor of Homer Simpson and family on the animated series. This guy could have been Ned's three-dimensional twin, and I wasn't the only person who thought so. Many people made comments to that effect. The sermon went on for about an hour and a half.

Although I don't remember getting much out of the sermons and not being able to concentrate on what was said, I kept going to church. I was hungry for God. I wanted to know what God wanted from me and what His purpose was for me on this earth. I wanted to feel love and acceptance, and I wanted to fill the void in my life. This was the void that was there even before I lost my friends and my wife. This was the void that longed to be filled by more than this world can offer. This was the void whose only rightful inhabitant is God.

Throughout the months I kept hanging out with Brent and his friends and going to worship services, revival meetings, and other church functions. Brent, his friend Dave, and I once went to a church in a nearby college town to hear a guest speaker by the name of John Stanton. I had never been to this church, nor did I know anyone there including the speaker. John Stanton was promoted as a prophet who foretold things about people by supernatural means. He was supposed to hear God's voice and speak His Words. I met John that day, and it was not the last time our paths would cross.

The church was probably one of the smallest church buildings I have ever entered. It was a little white building about the size of an old one room school house, and it was packed.

The service order was typical, with a time of worship and then the message. John delivered the message, and to tell you the truth I didn't get much out of it. As a matter of fact, the message was filled with jokes - bad jokes that weren't even funny. He would read a Scripture, say something about it, and then tell a joke. After that, he would pause and do what he called a "Holy Ghost Commercial." This so-called commercial consisted of him picking out someone in the crowd and giving them a word from God. I don't remember too much about the people he picked out or what he said to them. I just remember he must have done that at least ten times during his message. At one point he picked out a man who had bad teeth and he told the man his teeth were basically ugly, and he needed to quit eating sweets and get them fixed. Throughout the years I saw this guy he would often pick on people and say mean things. Looking back, I would say this guy was a bully and very arrogant.

After the service was over, he had people line up if they wanted a message from God. He sat in a chair at the front of the room with an assistant by his side. He would beckon a person to approach, and as they did John would hear from God on behalf of that person. He would share God's message with that person, and his assistant would write it down. Afterward, each person received a written record of their personal prophecy from Brother John.

When it was my turn, Dave and Brent came with me to the front of the church where this man was sitting. He was tall and clean-shaven with dark hair. I would say he was in his late forties to early fifties. He seemed to know a lot about me. He told me that I was having some marriage problems and financial problems. He even knew about the adultery issue. He asked where my wife is now, I said at home, and I told him she is having trouble finding a place to live. He then told me I had to throw her out that night and never take her back. He was very upset when he told me this, and he said I don't have to deal with a woman like that. He said that she needed to get out right now whether she had a place to go or not. It seemed that was the only message from God that he wanted to give me.

I asked him what my calling was or what kind of plan God had for my life. He replied with a very determined expression and said, "Never mind your calling or God's plan for you. The only thing you need to worry about is getting her out of your home and not taking her back." I was thinking, "What is this? The guy gave everyone else nice words from God and told them of how great a calling they had or how rich they will be, but all I get is a scolding about how I need to divorce my wife and throw her out." There is always the possibility that my friend told him about me, and that is how he knew what he knew. He did stay at my friend's mom's house on occasion when he was in the area to minister, and he kept in regular contact with my friend. However, he did seem to know some things that weren't generally known about my childhood that I hadn't told anyone. I also learned that Prophet John had been divorced a couple of times and one of his wives had become pregnant with a child that was not his. He divorced her and did not raise the child. Even if he wasn't a true prophet, at that time I believed he was, and I took his advice. I began taking steps to evict my wife from my house. Like I said that was not the last time I would see that prophet. I saw him throughout the years, and he was always inaccurate in his words from God for me. I had many problems with him, and he always put me down. I even got scammed out of several hundred dollars from him on a land investment scheme to feed starving children. At one point he told me very few people love me, and I will never be successful at anything. All words are supposedly from God. He had a large following though and spoke in a new church all around the country each night. He often brags how he takes in a million dollars a year; he lives in a mansion, and he is always doing some kind of scheme for money. He built a city for his orphans in Honduras and now the older ones he has working for him for cheap wages no doubt he is making money from their labor. This guy often puts down poor people and says he only wants to surround himself with successful people. He doesn't seem to be anything like Christ at all.

The next day I started trying to find a place for my wife to go. We tried most of her relatives, but they didn't want to take her in. She had no income or driver's license, so where was she to go? I was bound and determined to get her out as the prophet John had instructed me. It was breaking my heart to throw my pregnant wife out of my home though, but if that's what God wanted, I was trying to be obedient.

The night she left was very difficult for both of us. We had been arguing about her needing to find a place and we were both getting upset. I kept telling her our marriage was over, but she wasn't getting it. I finally told her, "It's time to leave," and she threw a temper tantrum. I thought that was a perfect opportunity to call the police and have them remove her. When the police arrived, she argued a little with them, and then she had a panic attack. Because she had a panic attack, the police were able to take her to the hospital. She ended up spending a day or two there in the psych unit, and then she went to stay with her mom. Again, I will say this was not easy for me. I was sorry it came to that, but it's what I felt I had to do at the time. Darcy was now out of my home, and I had done what I thought God wanted me to do. It was time for me to move on.

I felt like a great burden was lifted when my wife was gone. I felt the years of oppression and emotional abuse were over (she wasn't easy to get along with) and I didn't have to think about the adultery thing all the time. I felt that she was gone from my life never to hurt me again. I felt a lot better as I was free! I felt I could now move on, but feelings aren't always reliable. Things didn't go as planned. At this time, I was moving out of depression into a more manic state but of course still numb and in shock.

I continued to go to Church and hang out with Brent and Dave. But everyone seemed to hear that I was leaving my wife. I thought they would understand, but they didn't. Even though many knew the circumstances, I was still viewed as the bad guy. The consensus was that I was on my way to hell unless I took her back and raised those kids as my own. Over and over, it seemed like everywhere I looked I was being condemned. I went into the Church to find love and acceptance, but instead, I found judgment and condemnation. I was betrayed by the people closest to me. I didn't need condemnation. I needed love. In retrospect, the real shocker was that many of the people who told me I was going to hell and that God hates me were people who divorced their spouses for far less. Yes, I met many hypocrites in the Church who seemed to carry a Bible just so they could smack you with it.

I came into the Church expecting to find people who were real, people you could be honest with, people who loved God and shared His Love. Unfortunately, that's not what I found. To my dismay, I was wrong about that Church and the people in it. I had false expectations, and it took a long time to get over them. Even though those Christians acted the way they did, they weren't God. I wasn't going to hold it against Him. I decided to keep my faith, and I continued to pursue the One who pursued me regardless of how others acted. One thing I learned is divorce is the dirtiest word in the church and it is hated more than anything. It is actually viewed by many as an unforgivable sin.

I started to get even more serious about my faith. I continued to wonder what it was that God wanted from me, and what purpose He had for my life. I went to small group studies and more revival meetings, but now things were starting to sink in. At the church services I attended, I was starting to like the 40 minutes of worship, and I was actually starting to get something out of the sermons. The speakers used a lot of "Christianese," but as I learned about how Christians talked and acted, it got easier, and things started to click. I got hungrier and hungrier to learn about the word of God, and I even showed up for Church an hour early at times.

Then I started to read the Bible on my own time. All I had was an old King James Version, and it was kind of hard to understand. I remember asking people for help and trying to tell them that I didn't understand what it was saying. I asked them if there are Bibles that could explain things to me, but they weren't able to help me. As I look back on it now, I am amazed that in a church of over a hundred people no one seemed to know enough to tell me to get an easier translation or a Life Application Bible.

Whatever the reason, they were of no help at all. I was definitely on my own. I ended up going to a local bookstore and picking up a Life Application Study Bible that used the New Living Translation. It was so much better, and I understood what I was reading. Within months I switched to an NIV and then a NASB. The first book of the Bible I ended up reading was Exodus. I didn't read the gospels right away because I already knew them from when I went to Church as a child. So, Exodus it was, and I loved it. God spoke to me through it, and I became increasingly hungry for the Word. At first, I couldn't concentrate to read the Bible and tried an audio Bible, but I couldn't concentrate on that either. But over time as I learned to just keep reading everything over and over until understanding it and remembering it became easier. That helped and I could concentrate more on reading, but it was still hard. It was a struggle but my overwhelming hunger for it drove me to try my hardest. And I overcame that hurdle and now I have no trouble reading anything.

I continued to maintain a good relationship with my wife, who was still living with her mother at the time. Although we spent a lot of time together with our son Sam, I made it clear to her that our marriage was over and we were going to be divorced. So, our time together was more like friends spending time together than spouses. After she stayed with her mom for a while, her mom asked her to find a place of her own. I helped Darcy find an apartment, and it happened to be in the same apartment building that Lisa, a lady from church, lived in. Lisa was also my friend Dave's sister. Lisa reminded me a whole lot of the girl who Mandy Moore played on the movie "Saved." Lisa was one of the fakest Christians I knew. She was only in her twenties but was having Botox done to her face and liposuction to her body so she could look good in a bathing suit. She was little miss perfect (at least in her own mind) and acted like she was Mother Teresa. She put on an act like she was the most loving person who ever lived.

I remember the way Lisa prayed during prayer night at church. It was so fake that to this day I don't like going to longwinded prayer meetings. Her prayers had to be longer, louder, and have more emotion than anyone else's. It really makes you want to lose your lunch when you know it's just fake pageantry.

Lisa was the one who condemned me for not taking my wife back, even though she had divorced her husband. Lisa told me I was going to hell for not taking my wife back and raising the children as my own. She said that means I have a hard heart and hard-hearted people go to hell. In short, she was a classic hypocrite. She was always trying to get Darcy and I back together. She even started bringing Darcy to church on the nights she knew I would be there. I really didn't need that at the time. I needed to heal, and I needed God. I did not need all that constant condemnation and tricks – kindhearted or not - to reconcile our marriage. I believe Darcy understood, but Lisa, several other churchgoers, and a minister I would meet just didn't seem to get it.

There were others that I met who did the same things as Lisa. They would tell me just how much God hates divorce and will now hate me because I was getting one. They made divorce out to be some unforgivable sin, the sin that God hated the most. Over and over again I was bombarded with condemnation from people trying to tell me what to do, and using the Bible to beat me up. I didn't hear much about God loving me, or about His forgiveness, or that He has a plan for me. I only heard judgment.

Some people may agree. They may be saying, "Yes, stone him for throwing his pregnant wife out. Stone him for not taking her back and forgiving her. Stone him for not wanting to raise kids that aren't his." I can only say, "What if the shoe was on your foot? Should we stone you? Would there be no forgiveness for you? Would you raise your best friend's kids if the friend had an affair with your spouse and children were born out of it?" I didn't go out and have the affair. I didn't get my wife pregnant, yet I was treated by many in the faith community as though I was the one who had done wrong in the marriage.

But that's life. Sometimes things aren't as they should be - even in the Church. I don't believe that God was the One doing the condemning. If He was, He wouldn't be using hypocrites to do it. I learned that Christians are human, and this evangelical stuff may not be what it seems. Their actions didn't stop me from pursuing God. It did embitter me a little though, and it still baffles me how people can be so mean.

I started to share my faith more and more as I became hungrier for God. I wanted so badly to serve Him in some way, so I got an idea. It wasn't the best idea in the world, but it was something. I don't even recall how I came up with it, but I guess it was because I had some experience with it in the past. Years back my little brother had gotten an FM radio transmitter kit, and he would broadcast music on the FM band. It was very low power and maybe covered a city block. It was legal as long as the frequency you broadcast on is not already taken.

I decided I would start broadcasting Christian contemporary music in our city. I immediately sold my extra car (which I kind of regret because it was a really nice sports car) and I bought some radio broadcasting equipment. I purchased a radio transmitter, a 1-watt amp, and a large transmitting antenna. This came in a kit, and I had to put it together. When I say a kit, it was a kit all right. Basically, it was a blank circuit board with thousands of parts to solder in. It took several 8-hour days, but I managed to get it done and it actually worked.

With just the transmitter it was legal, and it roughly covered a city block. When I added the amp and the external transmitting antenna, I accidentally crossed the "legal" line. After the fact, I learned that I had become what is called a radio pirate. No, I didn't pillage or plunder, I didn't have an eye patch, and no one ever walked the plank. But that is what you call a person who broadcasts radio with more than a quarter watt of power without a license. The FCC doesn't really bother you if you only have one watt of power like I had, as long as you're not interfering with another station. As I look back on it now it was kind of a dumb thing to do, but it seemed like a good idea at the time.

So, I put it all together and started broadcasting. The signal actually reached the whole town that I lived in with a population of roughly 3,000, and the signal also reached the federal prison on the edge of town. It was really cool. We preached and witnessed on it, and we played the newest styles of contemporary music. I even bought an MP3 player which played thousands of songs randomly all day long. That was when MP3 players were much bigger and kind of a new thing. Once in a while, I would play a sermon from an evangelist who we had on tape or CD. At that time there was only one Christian station that was in the area and they only played the old hymns accompanied by an organ. So, we were filling a need in the area of contemporary Christian music. We had the radio station going for about 6 months until we ran into some trouble.

I was telling someone about the radio station and remarking that it would be nice to get a low-power FM license. They just happened to know the man who owned the local Christian radio station that only played the older hymns. They continued to tell me what a nice man he was, and they urged me to contact him and to ask for his help in getting a license. This was in a nearby town and it was not that far of a drive. I thought it would be nice to talk with him in person, so I drove to the radio station and asked for Mr. Laurence Stone.

Mr. Stone's secretary said he wasn't in at the time, but

she was able to dial his number and let me speak to him by phone from the office. He answered, and I introduced myself and proceeded to tell him what I was doing with my little radio station. I quickly found out he wasn't as nice as I was told. He actually got very upset and started yelling at me, "You're a radio pirate, and a criminal is what you are," he said. He was not helpful at all. On the contrary, he basically told me that I was in deep excrement.

After my conversation with Mr. Stone, I was expecting the FBI to show up with machine guns, jump out of helicopters onto the roof of our home and swing through our windows using grappling hooks and cable. The man was very graphic, and he spared no detail in telling me how the FBI will throw me in prison for the rest of my life and possibly shoot me. I asked him to help me do it legally, but he refused and even said he was going to turn me in.

A few weeks after talking with Mr. Stone I shut my station down and quit the radio business forever. I guess it was nice for a season, but all good things must end. I never heard from him again. The man was anything but nice, and after my experience with him I really didn't like his radio station much either. A couple of years later he passed away and his station was sold to a major Christian radio station that plays contemporary music.

It seemed like God was working in my life more and more each day, but I still did some of the same old things I did before I knew Him. I still watched bad movies, listened to bad music, swore, I had a bad smoking habit and many other things. I probably smoked 5 packs a day and then some. I could not be without a cigarette for even ten minutes. I loved smoking, and I had no plans to quit. Both of my parents smoked and all my friends smoked (before the church friends), so the bad habit didn't seem quite so bad.

But in the Church smoking was a filthy sin. People would make fake coughing noises and make all kinds of comments about my habit. They didn't seem to get too upset if somebody had a beer or a fifth of whiskey in their hand. As a matter of fact, a lot of Christians (including pastors) drink. But boy oh boy do they get upset over smoking. In any case, I still had some issues that I needed to deal with. I think the turning point came when an evangelist named Bill Keen came to our small Church. Bill was going to be holding revival meetings for two weeks, and did I ever need revival. My life was a mess. My mental illness was also still a problem and I hated taking pills for my disorder.

I remember the first night Bill spoke at our Church. I sat in the second pew. I was hungry for God and hungry for whatever this revival thing was about. This time it was different. God was about to get my attention in a supernatural way. I would remember this service for the rest of my life.

It started like any other service until the message part. The speaker came out and told us a little about himself. He was in his early forties with an average build and height, and he had spiked hair. He said he was from California, and I think he said he had five or six children. When he started to preach, it was different this time than any other church service or revival meeting I had ever attended. I was able to pay attention and every time he made a point, he would walk right over to me, point at me, and say my name. He would say "Adam, I am talking to you." This went on throughout the whole message, challenging people to live a Godly life.

I couldn't believe the nerve of this guy. I hated being singled out. It was embarrassing, but I also liked the challenge at the same time. I certainly got something out of this sermon. Boy did I ever. How could I not? The sermon was personalized for me. I went to him afterward and asked him why he said my name and pointed to me all the time. His reply was, "I don't know what you're talking about. I never did that at all, not even once." Doubting him, I asked my friends and they replied the same way. They said they "never heard my name at all." I couldn't believe it, but I know what I saw and heard.

"God must have truly been speaking through him," I thought as I drove home that night. I couldn't believe that God would do that, but He did. It seemed God was speaking to me, and He wanted me to get my act together. That night I quit smoking cold turkey and never picked it up again. I quit everything else I knew I was doing to hinder the Spirit at that time too. My walk would be genuine from that point forward. I knew that God was real at that moment, and no one could convince me otherwise. I wanted nothing more than to please Him. It seemed God wanted my obedience and my full attention, and now He had it. I now look back on it and that experience wasn't really affirming that Christianity was true or right but that I needed to live a cleaner life. I needed to live a little more moral life and quit doing some things that were not only bad for my spiritual health but also bad for my physical health as well.

Adam Lee

Evangelical Christianity Is A Cult

Chapter 3

Reconciled

It was during Bill Keen's two-week revival meetings that I decided to take my wife back and raise the twins as my own. After God got my attention the first night, I had to keep going back to all of the meetings. I remember trying to talk to this man who God used, and it didn't go so well. When he asked me if I had a family, I told him what had happened in my marriage. He basically told me that God hates divorce and that I should take her back and raise those kids. He then distanced himself from me and treated me like some kind of an outcast.

Bill also kept asking me if I was really getting anything out of his meetings. It just seemed to me like this guy did not like me very much and that he was judging me over the marriage thing. He would talk to the others all the time with a smile on his face, but with me there was no smile. I got the feeling that he just didn't want to talk with me. My two friends Dave and Brent were his favorites. Brent and Dave would go out and party and claim to "witness" to the girls that they were sleeping with. At church the next day, Bill would call them up front to preach about living a Godly life and being the Church in the world. It was like Bill was blind to everyone else's issues but mine.

I did my best to put those feelings aside. Whether Bill liked me or not, it seemed God was using him to speak to me. I wanted to hear what he said in his services, and I was interested in seeing what God would do next. It was all a blur from that point. All I remember is that my heart was really changing through these meetings.

I remember falling on my face on the altar, lying on the floor with my arms stretched out to God during the worship portion of the service and crying out, "Lord, I surrender to you." I just couldn't get enough worship. My heart yearned for more of God. I would have died for Him and did anything He asked. God saved me and set me free from so much, and I wanted to serve Him in any way I could. He became everything to me. I would have traded the whole world for Him. That was what seemed to be the main message that revival ministers would teach is to surrender your whole life and be willing to die for Christ. To be set ablaze for Him and be obedient.

After those first few revival services, I was always praying and worshiping God, at home, in the car, even in the store and at work. God taught me that you can be filled with His Spirit and Presence anywhere, any time. You just have to believe it, have an open yielding heart and receive it. You don't need some fancy revival meeting. You don't need a pastor to lay hands on you. You just need an open yielding heart and faith. From that point on, I started to feel the Presence of the Lord almost everywhere I went. I was developing a lifestyle of being in Him.

With God's Presence in my life, I was overcoming all that once held me in bondage. All the sin, hurt and problems were fading into gray. But I still dealt with temptation and spiritual attacks. I remember one time I was taking an afternoon nap on the couch at my home. I was just dozing off when the phone rang. I reached over on the arm of the couch and picked up my phone. There was a strange, evil-sounding voice on the other end. It said, "Your time is up. I am going to get you," and then hung up. I thought, "What is this all about? Whatever..." I then put down the phone and went back to sleep. After a short while, I woke up and went to visit my mom.

As my mom and I spoke, I told her about the weird phone call I received that may have been a dream. She was shocked and said, "That's amazing. I had a similar dream about a half an hour ago while I was taking a nap." In her dream, the phone rang. When she answered, an evil voice on the other end said, "I want Adam. I am going to kill him." I couldn't believe it and still don't believe it. It seemed like Satan or one of his demons was actually trying to scare me, and he wasn't being discrete about it. He came right out and called me and attempted to terrorize my mother.

* * *

My life was changing for the better, and I was feeling better. The void in my life was being filled by my new best friend named Jesus Christ, who was and is better than any friend I could ever imagine. At least the real version of Him is the evangelical version not so much. At that point, I was still separated from my wife and still under condemnation from fellow believers. But that was about to change. It was during the last night at the revival meeting that I decided to take my wife back.

Again, I worshiped with all my heart and wholeheartedly took in the message. During the message, the minister came over to me and said you are free. I was thinking free from what. Then something spoke to my heart and said, "What do you want to be free of?" and I thought of anxiety, depression, and having to take pills. So, I thought it was so. I was healed of my mental issues right then and there. I was so happy and was so in love with God that I wanted to do something for Him, after all, He opened my eyes and took away the darkness. He just healed me of mental health issues, so I had to do something significant for Him. I just didn't want to live like I always lived before. I wanted to make my whole life count for Him, every minute of every day. During one of the final songs that night I vowed to God that I would take my wife back and raise those children as my own. I knew in my heart that they weren't mine biologically, but I vowed before God that they would be mine from now on in my heart. I didn't do this because of the pressure and condemnation. I didn't do this because I didn't want to be alone or because I loved my wife. I did this for God, I thought that is what He wanted. After all, even a minister was telling me if I didn't do it I was going to hell. I would make this sacrifice for Him as He had sacrificed for me. And it was so!

I felt good about the whole thing and was at peace with my decision. I had the plan all laid out in my mind. I was going to take my wife back, she would be grateful, and we would live happily ever after. But that isn't how it turned out. Things never turn out the way they are planned. That's just how it goes. But looking back on it I am happy it didn't go as planned, for if it had I wouldn't have matured as much or grown as close to God through the process.

So, I took Darcy back and I moved her back into my home. She was about 8 months pregnant with the twins and was soon to pop! Things were not easy when I left, and while I was gone things got worse. Darcy taught our son to call me all kinds of swear words. He was only two years old, but he had a mouth like a sailor. I remember displeasing him while we were at Walmart one day, and my two-year-old son said, "F#!* off, Daddy!" loud enough for everyone and their brother to hear. Can you imagine some of the looks people gave me?

Darcy also taught Sam some other things like, "Daddy, you're a F!#*ing loser," and all kinds of other profanities and insults. It made me feel low. My two-year-old son was saying horrible things. He was just repeating the things he heard his mom call me, but it wasn't right. What could I do in the middle of Walmart, but try and ignore him and keep walking. Of course, we cut our shopping trip short and headed for the door.

My wife grew up in a house where it was normal for her mom to call her dad or some other man a loser or worthless. She would call him profanities on a regular basis, and it was normal for profanities and insults to fly for little or no reason in Darcy's family. I remember one time my wife had a run-in with a police officer. This guy had been a police officer for many years, and he told me that he had never heard a woman spit out profanities and insults like her in his whole life. I told him if he thinks that's bad he should hear the things she calls me all the time. I was able to smooth things over and get her out of trouble, but only because the officer felt sorry for me.

This definitely was not an easy time for us. Darcy was not openly grateful for me taking her back and raising the twins as my own. Right from the start, there were all kinds of problems. But I was still kind of happy I was healed of mental health issues and I went off my meds.

Not long after I took Darcy back an evangelist by the name of Taylor Strom visited our Church. He too would be doing revival services for a couple of weeks. I could feel that God wanted to take me to a deeper level, and I felt that some significant things were about to happen through this visiting ministry. I made sure I was the first one in the door at his meeting, showing up my usual hour early. The first few nights he gave his testimony and talked about how he would also be teaching us to share our faith. He went on and on about how he used to pray four hours a day, was an elder in his Church, used to be rich and successful and had it all together until one day God showed him that it was all meaningless. It was all for show and self-indulgence. Nothing was of the heart, and God was calling him to touch people's lives outside the church walls through personal evangelism and discipleship. He had been too comfortable with his life, all his possessions, and the outward appearance of being a pillar in the Church. He had failed to see that there is a world full of hurting people on their way to hell. I loved it when he threw out all of the ritualistic garbage in the Church and focused on the Gospel and the way Christ ministered to people. He encouraged people to take off the masks they wear and to be real.

The Lord spoke to me a lot as I sat through these services. He spoke to me about my life and my calling and all kinds of other things. The Lord made it clear that I was called to ministry, but I had no idea what type of ministry. Was it evangelistic, apostolic, pastoral, helps, or the prophet? This was a charismatic Church, so the office of the prophet was believed to still be functional and valid.

God wasn't making it clear what ministry I was called to, but at least I had a general direction. I knew that I was called to ministry, and I started to pursue preparation for that calling.

The second night was a little different. Something unique was going to take place but I didn't know it. Darcy and I had been praying for a week for some financial deliverance, as we were out of everything from food to toilet paper. We needed money and we needed it fast. We had prayed and prayed, and there just seemed to be no answer. While I was sitting in the service that night and listening to the minister speak I felt the Holy Spirit put on my heart to get up, leave the service, and go witness to people on the streets. I thought, "What is that all about? I can't do that. I don't even know how." I fought the Holy Spirit for about five minutes until I finally gave in. I didn't tell anyone what I was going to do. I only told my wife I had to run outside for something and I would be right back.

I got up and left the church, and headed up to Main Street a block away. It must have been about 8:30 to 9:00 PM by then. I walked right up to the first group of people I saw. They happened to be a group of about fifteen teenagers standing on Main Street talking about Lord knows what. I walked right up to them and I slammed them with the Gospel, asking them if they knew the Lord and telling them they needed Jesus. They became upset immediately and shot me down in flames. They asked me why people from my church are always bothering them, and why we can't just leave them alone.

So I left them alone and traveled south down Main Street trying to talk to the people who passed by. None of them wanted to hear what I had to say either. I even went to a gas station and stopped cars as they were leaving, knocking on their window asking them if they would go to heaven if they were to die tomorrow. Some thought about it while the majority didn't care. It seemed to me like this whole street preaching thing was not working so well. I called it a night and walked back to the church feeling like a failure.

At the time I theorized that it wasn't the Holy Spirit or God that led me to leave the church and go preach that night. I thought that maybe it was the devil, and he tricked me so that I would miss something good at the service. I was certain that when I returned the minister would hear from God, and that he would rebuke me for being such an idiot and listening to the devil.

I made it back to church and the service was still going on. I returned to my seat with my head down, believing that I would be rebuked. But after sitting there for a few minutes nothing happened. Then all of a sudden the speaker pointed at me and said, "You, come up here." I was scared out of my boots. This was just what I was afraid of. This man was going to tell everyone that I hear from the devil, and he was going to rebuke me - or worse, excommunicate me.

I decided to go up there anyway, and if that was what he was going to do I was going to take it like a man. I stood up and made my way to the front of the church with my head held high ready for my rebuke. The man moved to the side of me and put his arm around me and had me face the congregation. I thought, "Oh no, here it comes. Please don't let this happen, Lord. Please, not in front of everyone." The minister began to speak and he said, "Look at this young man. He gets it. The Lord says, 'This is a man after my own heart. He is called.' Watch this man's life and see what happens with it. God is pleased."

Then he prayed over me, and without me ever telling him or anyone else at the church that we had a financial need, he took up an offering for us. I didn't know what to say. I was so shocked and amazed, it was all so hard to grasp. God is so good. Just when you think that all is lost He surprises you. I thought for sure I heard from the devil. I thought for sure God was not going to answer our prayer, but I was wrong. After he took the offering he gave us the money, and it was over a thousand dollars! I couldn't believe it. It was enough to meet our needs and then some. We gave what we didn't need to the Church and to Taylor Strom Ministries. We were so blessed. I learned that it didn't matter whether or not the people I witnessed to accepted what I said. It wasn't even about Christianity being right or about preaching to anyone. It was about me having a relationship with God that is what was important.

During those revival meetings, my life changed more and more. I was starting to come out of my shell and develop more personal self-confidence as a Christian. I ended up going to some of the evangelism training classes, and I loved it. They provided a script for starting conversations and witnessing to people. Starting the conversation is the hardest part for most people, but the script simplified all that. The classes and the evangelism training gave me the confidence to just go up to anyone at any time and start talking to them about Jesus.

I dove right in and went to every outreach available.

There were outreaches in a few different towns, and I was at all of them. They were all organized the same way. We would all meet at a church in that town, and we would go out in teams of two or three walking the streets and using the script with the people we met.

Basically, we walked up to people and told them that God loves them and has a plan for their life. We asked them if they were to die today, would they go to heaven? We then explained to them that the wages of sin is death and that all have fallen short of the Glory of God. We then explained that Christ died for their sins, and if they believed that and prayed a prayer with us they would be welcomed in heaven. It worked well, and I personally prayed with and led hundreds of people to Christ. It was really easy and fun, and these people walked away thinking that they were now going to heaven.

It made us feel good, and we hoped that it changed the lives of those we engaged with for the better. But the truth was that most of the lives we touched through this ministry didn't change at all, and they really weren't going to heaven. I felt pretty good about it at the time, but in retrospect, I didn't really do a whole lot of good.

I am convinced now that many people just prayed with us to get us to leave them alone. But at the time I didn't realize any of this, and I was on cloud nine thinking that we were doing such great things for the Lord's work.

One thing I did notice about Christianity that I didn't really get was they always scared people with the fear of burning in hell which was death and torture. Of course, it was death and torture in the next life after you die here on earth, but it was none the less death and torture. I just loved God and didn't really care to think about fearing burning in hell and being tortured for all eternity. But that is the Christian message you turn or burn. A very classic sign of a cult. If this was a new idea that just came about and some little religious group of people on the other side of town started saying this, they would be labeled a dangerous cult and run out of town. I think we are too comfortable with Christianity that we just can't see how much of a cult it really is.

* * *

There was something else that occurred in that church revival meeting that will forever stay with me. Partly as a learning experience and partly as a shocker of just how bad Evangelicals can be.

I was at one of the revival meetings and I went up front in a line of people standing to get prayed for. The common belief and custom was that the power of God hits you where you are standing and knocks you down. Usually there is someone behind you to catch you as you fall backward to the floor but sometimes there isn't, and people just fall. So, the minister waved his hand and said the power of God touch you and I felt emotion and fall back as was what was common. Only I didn't have anyone behind me to catch me. I went straight back and on my way to the ground my head connected with a hard wooden church pew! My neck twisted and I settled on the floor. I was still conscious but when I tried to see I noticed that my vision was not working.

I could only see little bright dots all over kind of like

stars on a dark night. I was blind! I told the ministers there and they laughed and said that I was going to be fine. I got very scared at this point and begged them to take me to the hospital emergency room. The pastor refused and said, "be healed in Jesus' name." I was not instantly healed and still was blind and continued to ask to be taken to the hospital, but they kept saying that God has you and you will be fine. Finally, after the church service was over a friend of mine took me to the hospital. By the time I arrived my vision was coming back. I doctor said the place my head hit the pew controlled my sight and that is why I could not see. I ended up having a concussion for a few days but recovered. Everything turned out OK, but they should have taken me to the emergency room! I am sure they were breaking some laws not to mention being complete assholes. I could have died. This was not a good experience and throughout my time in Christianity, little things would happen like this quite often.

After that, I continued to preach to everyone everywhere. I preached in stores, at family get-togethers, and even on the beach. One time we went to a bowling alley that had a bar connected to it. This was way before I had evangelism training, but even back then I had a hunger to share my faith. This took place in February, in Wisconsin. This particular night the temperature was twenty-five degrees below zero. It was a Church fellowship fun night, and I rode with a couple of friends.

We all went in and were getting ready to bowl and then I said, "I've got an idea - let's go witness a little." They agreed and we were off. My friend Brent was in the lead, and he led us straight into the bar area and right up to a couple of heavyset women in their forties. Brent immediately asked them the first line of the script and said, "If you were to die today do you know if you would go to heaven or not?"

The lady on my left side became furious. She started yelling, "We have had problems with people like you before." She then stated that she was the owner's girlfriend, and she called out to the bartender saying, "These guys are preaching in here. Throw them out!" I told her she needs Jesus, and we started for the entryway back into the bowling alley. The bartender ran after us. He tried to ask my friends if they were preaching, but they ran too quickly. I was last so it wasn't too hard for him to catch up to me. He grabbed my arm and asked "Were you preaching in here?" I answered him, "Yes, I was." The man then said, "You are out of here," and he escorted me outside of the building and told me to never come back.

I sat out in the parking lot while my friends stayed another 3 hours and bowled. Remember, the temperature that night was a bone chilling twenty-five degrees below zero and I was 50 miles from home. I assumed it was "one for all and all for one" when it came to brothers in Christ, but that wasn't the case. Not even the pastor of our Church who encouraged us to witness came to my aid. I learned that some professing Christians are very much like everyone else. So it was that I sat in the cold to pay for my "crime." It was quite an experience, and the first bar I was ever thrown out of for preaching (but not the last).

In the summer of that year, after all of our evangelism training, we went to an evening conference at a nearby church. After the conference I said to my friends, "Hey, let's go and do some preaching somewhere," as I was all fired up from the conference. Dave said, "That's sounds great, and I know just the place." So we walked downtown and followed him into a bar, only to find that the bar was filled with people from the church that we had just left. Let's just say I was surprised, and I sat there pretty bored while my friends drank and mingled. At least I didn't get thrown out this time. I only stayed for about ten minutes before I left the bar and went home. This time I had my own car nearby and it was summer, so I didn't freeze to death like the last time. But I learned that Christianity is not what it seems. People can be in church condemning everyone and everything one minute, then in the bar the next living it up and doing the things they were condemning.

I can remember another time I was out witnessing that I will never forget. We went out in groups and I ended up sharing the Gospel with a young woman who worked at the fruit stand on Main Street. She accepted Jesus as her personal Lord and Savior right there at the fruit stand. I later saw my friend Brent, and he asked me how the outreach went today. I told him about the people I prayed with, and when I mentioned the girl on Main Street he took great interest. He said, "You prayed with the hot girl at the fruit stand?" It seemed that he knew a little about her, or least had his eye on her. I said, "I sure did and she accepted Christ." He said, "Hey let's go around town and do some more preaching." I said, "Yes, that's a great idea."

Brent instructed me to go down two blocks to the right and he would go down to two blocks to the left. So I did, and I went door to door for a little while and then circled back around to Main Street only to find that he was talking to the girl at the fruit stand. If I were a betting man I'd bet that he didn't go evangelizing at all. Instead, he probably went right over to the fruit stand and proceeded talking the "hot" girl into a date with him. She ended up going on a few dates with him, and then my other friend Dave also started asking her out. After a while they were fighting over her and taking her to drinking parties and all kinds of other things that Christians don't usually go to. When it was all said and done, I heard that she was telling people she wants nothing more to do with God - and especially our Church.

My friends were good at that. They seemed to share the Gospel and witness to a lot of people, but it always seemed to be women. And then they would date these women and call it "discipleship." I remember Dave would always say he had a gift to heal people. But that also seemed to be only directed towards women. He would often tell me how he healed girls by the laying on of hands. He would tell how he would touch their back or some other part of their body where they were in pain, rub them and it would go away. He would then proceed in telling me how he had dated her.

It was clear that my friends were using this evangelism thing as a pick-up line, and using the healing thing to molest women. This was wrong. I confronted them on this, but it didn't do any good.

As I look back on Brent and Dave, I can see that they had some serious issues. I don't see them much anymore, but I can tell you that life has beaten them up and matured them some. While I don't condone doing some of the things they did, I am grateful that they encouraged me to come to Church and even hung out with me outside the

Church when I would have otherwise been alone.

Besides my new love for evangelism, I also learned to step out in faith more. I started to give to those that had need. It was rewarding and I loved it. Even though I had needs, it felt so good to help others. I also learned that when we give we don't covet and hoard things as much, as the Spirit tends to remove materialism from our heart. I even ended up giving away my only car to someone who needed one. I figured that I would just buy a new one or God would provide. He actually did provide. About two weeks later someone gave us a van. This was just what we needed anyway, as our car would have been too small for three car seats and my wife and I. So it worked out well. Although the giving message was often abused in the churches I went to. The evangelists would say to give it all till it hurts. The churches would say if you don't tithe ten percent of your income each week then you are robbing God and you will be under a curse. They quote scripture and all but knowing what I know now this is wrong. This was yet another red flag of a cult, I would not realize it though and go on to give the church a lot of my finances. God doesn't need your money as one mentor in my life will tell you and most churches just use the money to fatten their own pockets. If you are in need and go to them for help, they don't help you and will just tell you to find a better paying job and don't be lazy. Most evangelicals are republican, and most republicans don't believe in helping poor people or giving away money except giving it to the church.

Throughout this time other things happened. I began to pursue my calling to ministry even though I didn't know where exactly it would lead me. I remember having dreams all the time. Some of these dreams were supernatural, revealing things to me about other people. Besides having dreams, I started to hear God's voice a lot clearer for me and others. It was like I had some kind of close connection to God.

I had a dream about a lady in our Church. In my dream, she showed me her stomach which happened to have a tumor or large growth in it. She was concerned over this. I ended up asking her about this when I saw her. Sure enough, she had been praying to God for help. She did have a growth and she needed to have it removed. She had not told anyone at the church about it yet, especially me. She said there was no way I could have known, except by God. I thought it was kind of cool and it made going to sleep and dreaming a whole lot more exciting. Ever since then I learned all I could about dream interpretation, and I got quite good at it. I went through a lot of Christian dream interpretation classes and I read a lot of books on the subject. If God was going to use dreams to speak to me, I wanted to be prepared and know what they meant.

I learned that God used dreams to speak to people throughout the Old and New Testaments, and He still uses them today. One thing I learned about dreams is that we must have faith and believe that He can speak to us in that manner. I talked to a man once who had taken a psychology course at a local college. He said that the class taught him all about dreams and where they came from. He held the popular academic belief that dreams are simply a product of our mind. In short, he said dreams don't have any meaning and they are useless. I asked him, "How often did you dream before you took the class?" He said, "I dreamt all the time." I then asked, "How often did you dream after you took the class?" He said, "I actually stopped dreaming." It is obvious that his faith wasn't there anymore. His belief that dreams don't mean anything affected his ability to dream. In any case, my faith level was up and I was ready for God to speak to me in any way He chose. In any case, I kept having dreams that would reveal to me things about people I couldn't possibly know by natural means, and when I would tell them they would be shocked and some would even get upset. My dreams would even warn me of things in the future for my life. Things like someone lying about me and coming against me and all kinds of other things. I sure valued my dreams in those days that was for certain and I still value them today.

Life kept moving, and before long the twins were born. They were born in August, and we knew the date they would be born because my wife was having them via Cesarean section. It was about 8:00 AM when my wife gave birth to the twins at our town hospital. Paul was first, and then Isaac. Paul was the bigger of the two, weighing in at seven pounds fourteen ounces, while Isaac was six pounds fifteen ounces. They were about a minute apart, but aside from their size, you could hardly tell them apart. They weren't identical twins, but they sure looked alike. To this day it is still hard to tell those two apart.

Oh, the joy of having twins. What a job it was raising two babies at once. If I wasn't there to help, I don't know how my wife could have done it. We already had one still in diapers and now there were two more. But she almost didn't keep them. Before I took Darcy back, a lady at our church was trying to get her to give the twins to some wealthy couple. The couple supposedly had loads of money, and the twins would have had the finest upbringing money could buy. The woman kept telling us the rich couple would be able to raise the twins much better than we ever could. She was oddly persistent, and she would not take "no" for an answer. We later found out that she was going to likely receive a very lucrative "finder's fee" if my wife agreed to give the twins away. God had different plans though. That same woman was supposed to be some kind of minister and had an outreach. She got all the stuff from the thrift store outreach for free and bragged about helping so many poor souls. She claimed she didn't do it for the money but did it for the Lord. Funny thing was when the twins were born I went to her store to buy cribs and all kinds of other baby items. She knew we were dirt poor and yet she did not give us the items for free, she didn't even give us a discount. Yes, we sure felt her charity to the community and good works that she bragged about.

We may not have been rich, but God was going to provide for the children just as much as that couple could have. I couldn't imagine that the couple would have loved the twins any more than we do.

After the twins were born it was hard. It is hard enough getting up with one child in the middle of the night, but two was nearly unbearable. When one awoke so did the other. When they both awoke, their crying would wake our oldest child. For the first couple of months, we hardly slept a wink. It was unbelievably crazy, and with no sleep, it sometimes seemed like some kind of a bad dream. It took both of us to meet the demands of those two babies, and then some. I really didn't do a whole lot with our firstborn, but with the twins, I was involved with everything. You would think that this kind of stress would really affect my mental health issues and me being off my meds but it didn't. I was a trooper and did very well. The mental health didn't seem to be a problem anymore. And my doctor took notice. He said there must have been some kind of miracle because I was doing well. Eventually, he quit being my doctor because I didn't need one but he remained my good friend.

We did continue to have marriage trouble throughout the years and I tried over and over again to reach out for help from people in my Church. I remember telling people about my situation, and all they would say was that my wife was acting the way she did because "I wasn't loving enough. If I was more loving she would straighten right up." Basically, it was my fault according to them. In their eyes, it seemed like I was still the bad one for not wanting to take her back or raise those kids. Again, many of the people who gave this advice were divorced, and most of those divorces were not for irreconcilable differences. As I look back on it, these were not the people I should have been asking for advice. I still can't believe that there weren't better people around me who were willing to help me. I just wasn't ever good enough for the people in churches. I just did not fit in. They were always criticizing and condemning me for whatever they could. I certainly got beat down a lot.

I even sought help from my pastor, but he really wouldn't talk to me much about it either. He had been divorced two years earlier, and he had many of the same problems with his wife as I was having with Darcy. It must have been too close to home for him, as he had no comment on the things that I was going through. Our Church had some problems also. We were in the middle of a new building program that we couldn't afford, and the pastor was under criticism for his divorce from some of the congregation. He seemed to be too preoccupied with those things to even provide me with a "listening ear." Besides the advice I got from all the hypocrites, I was on my own. So I put up with it and tried to love Darcy the best I could, relying on God's Presence and Comfort to see me through.

Not long after the twins were born, I signed up for a Correspondence Bible College that was offered through my Church. My pastor knew the school, and he gave me a good reference. Of course, there was tuition and other expenses, but my psychiatrist offered to cover my costs. He became a friend of the family who was kind of like a father to me. My father had been out of my life for the most part since I was a teenager, so this man stepped in to help guide me. Dr. Friend as I call him even taught me how to drive and helped me get my license when I was sixteen. My father said I was too stupid to drive a car. My doctor let me use his car to practice driving, and even to take the road test. I was so happy to be enrolled in a Bible school. I was actually making visible progress toward my calling. I still didn't know what ministry I was called to, but this school would help me explore them all. I was also excited to learn more about the Bible. And even though it was hard at first I could now concentrate and focus. Things were certainly getting better.

The school was a Word-of-Faith, Spirit-filled Charismatic Bible College. I learned all kinds of practical things through the school, and it challenged me to grow in my spiritual life and my daily walk with the Lord. The classes I took on prayer were interesting. The classes taught me to be sensitive to the leading of the Holy Spirit in prayer, and to let Him show me who and what to pray for. It really worked. Rather than having a big list or something on my mind, when I go to the Lord in prayer, I just ask Him to show me what to pray for. And He does.

One time in prayer the Lord gave me a vision of a girl I knew who had a knife over her. She was crying and depressed. I prayed for God to protect her and deliver her from harm. The next day I saw her and asked her about it. She said she was depressed and suicidal that night, but that she was feeling better and her depression had passed. Things like that were always coming to me through prayer, and I had to learn to let go of my own agenda for God to show me His Agenda for me. In that way, the school and the classes were great. There were also a lot of doctrinal, legalistic things at the school that seemed to stifle the Spirit. With God's help I learned to "chew on the cherries and spit out the pits."

Also around that time I got involved with the Full Gospel Business Men's Association. My friend Dave introduced me to them, and it seemed like a perfect fit for me. They loved to evangelize. I ended up speaking at a few of their meetings and helping out for a couple of years at a booth they call the God Mobile. The God Mobile was really neat. It was a concessions trailer that was outfitted as a portable booth to set up and evangelize at county fairs. The booth had a sign that asked, "Are you going to heaven? Answer two questions to find out."

The people who would come to the God Mobile were invited to fill out a form with two questions on it. The first question was, "Are you going to heaven?" with a yes or no selection. Most people checked yes. The second question was: "If yes, why?" This was a multiple-choice question, with many answers such as: "I obey the Ten Commandments," or "I am a good person," and even "Because I go to church." If they didn't answer, "Because I have a personal relationship with Jesus," that would open the door for us to explain salvation via the "Roman Road." We would explain how that works and prayer aren't sufficient, and there is no way to earn your way into heaven. The only way into heaven is through a personal relationship with Jesus Christ. I prayed with hundreds of people and led them to Christ through the God Mobile.

They seemed to worship Christ more than God, while Jesus was also believed to be lower than God and part human they still exalted him above God. I never really felt right about this. It was always Jesus this and Jesus that. This was certainly a cult sign as having a strong devotion to a man or figure.

* * *

Some people told me that I was not called to ministry and that I was not good enough.

These people and the Bible seemed to strive for perfection, I knew that everyone else wasn't perfect and we were all human, so this didn't make sense to me. Yet that is what Christianity seems to believe and what the Bible seems to say. This was also a red flag of a cult, but I never would have thought it at the time. At that time, you couldn't tell me much of anything. I was on a mission, a mission from God or so I thought.

I later learned that there are many generations of

pastors on my father's side of the family. It looked as though being a pastor was the family trade. I had great-grandfathers who were Presbyterian, Lutheran, and even Evangelical Free pastors. After learning that I was pursuing ministry, my grandfather gave me his father's handwritten sermon notes. I couldn't believe it. I came from such a long line of pastors, and now it seemed God was leading me to follow in their footsteps. My father never talked about his grandfather or any of the family history, so this was a very pleasant surprise for me. This was one of the greatest confirmations to my calling I thought. No matter what others said, I thought then that I was truly called to ministry and I was going to keep working toward it.

A several-month internship with a working pastor was a requirement of my Bible College program. My Pastor agreed to mentor me, and I was very excited. Unfortunately, my excitement didn't last very long. One morning my pastor made a sobering announcement to the congregation. It turned out he had been having some health issues for months. Something was wrong with his throat. He had it examined by a specialist, and the tests confirmed he had ALS (Amyotrophic Lateral Sclerosis, also known as Lou Gehrig's disease, or motor neuron disease). ALS is a life-threatening disease with no cure and a life expectancy of three years. I was shocked.

This was a charismatic Church that believed in healing. Pastor Tom was a graduate of Oral Roberts University, known for its founder and namesake who gained international fame as a faith healer. How could my pastor be dying from a disease? He was only 44 years old. This was crazy. "He will surely be healed," I thought to myself. His condition worsened quickly, and a few weeks later he informed me that he would be taking an indefinite leave of absence. The internship was over.

Tom told me that I could most likely finish my internship at our "Sister Church" 30 miles away. I couldn't believe it. "This can't be happening," I thought to myself. I asked God, "How and why? Why are You letting this man die, this pastor who serves You and preaches that You are a healer of all? Why are You letting him die by such a cruel disease?" God has not yet answered me. I am still asking, "Why? Why God? What kind of witness was that?"

* * *

Tom ended up dying about 5 years later. Some say it was God's punishment for Pastor Tom's sin, others attribute his death to a lack of faith, but who can say. If it was sin, then we all better look out. I watched Tom's life closely and I kept in contact with him. Until the day he died, Tom still believed he would be healed. This man did not lack faith. Most of the people who offered spiritual reasons for his death were the same ones who had condemned me. Only God knows all the answers.

When Pastor Tom left our Church, the board found an interim pastor. Eventually, this split the Church, and the majority of the Church joined another Church in town. This left only a handful of people at the Church, burdened with a building program they couldn't afford before the split, let alone now. The remaining Church persevered. Several years later they started to grow again, and they have since moved into their new building.

Christianity seemed to be against knowledge and

reason and were prone to delusions. Just look at some of the nonsense they believe and how they are against logic and science. Christianity actually hates science, and the bible speaks against knowledge and reason. All the marks of a cult.

Chapter 4

Changed or Not Changed

The "Sister Church" where I finished my internship was different. The pastor was even more charismatic than my former pastor, Tom. At one time this Church was an Assembly of God congregation. They eventually changed their affiliation to become a Word of Faith congregation. The worship lasted longer and seemed to be even more anointed than the worship at my home Church. The people at this Church also seemed to have a more emotional experience than my home Church. The Church had all kinds of things going on. They even spent New Year's Eve together.

Pastor Greg and his wife were so kind that they would let people who had no place to go actually stay in their home or live at the Church. His sermons were livelier. It seemed like God was truly there.

Although I started to notice a strict mandate at this church as well as other churches to submit to leadership no matter what. I found this to be a thing not only in the churches I went to but all over Christianity. They used scripture from the Bible to affirm this. I often wondered if this was right or not? How could you submit to their leadership and do what they told you even if it seemed wrong? What about God, isn't doing what God wanted you to do more important than church leadership and submitting to a man? This never sat well with me, and I actually saw a lot of bad things come out of people submitting to the church hierarchy. This was one of the red flags of a cult but at the time I had no clue.

My wife didn't seem to like it there though, and she didn't get anything out of it. Even when they would provide us with childcare so she could focus on worship, she still wasn't happy. She was always angry about something. The whole half-hour ride to church would consist of her yelling and cursing at me and the kids.

One of the first things I did was to set some rules about our friends and the people we were surrounding ourselves with. Our marriage had been affected by a whole lot of friends who were not Godly. Many of these friends abused drugs and alcohol. I insisted that we sever our ties with these types of friends and that we become very selective in making new friends with solid Christian values. I also set several other rules. Because of our history with adultery in our marriage, I also made it a rule that neither one of us would allow a situation where we would be alone with the opposite sex. I also insisted that we sever relationships with immoral friends, and even distance ourselves from family members that practiced immorality.

I even insisted that we stop watching ungodly and negative movies. We would put God first in all things, and start loving people instead of being rude to them. We would also start agreeing on parenting our children and raising them up as Christians who are polite and love the Lord.

It all felt good, I stepped up to take the ***lead*** position as the head of the house.

I explained to my wife that our marriage is most likely not going to work if we don't change things and try these rules. I reminded her that I am trying to make it work, and if she wanted it to work, we would have to start doing things differently. We would have to start doing things God's way. She agreed, and we made the rules official.

In a perfect world that would have solved our problems. In reality, it didn't go so well

During this time, it seemed like God continued to do miracles in our lives and bless us. Early on I was taking a faith study course and it said to remind God of His word and kind of name it and claim it. So, I did, I believed and proclaimed that I would be blessed right now a hundred times what I have blessed others. Well two weeks after that my friend called and said his brother died and he wanted me to help get things from his brother's house and he would give me some stuff. So I helped him and I was given men's gold jewelry, electronics, a new motorcycle, an SUV, a real Rolex watch and then a couple months later he bought us a house.

I was also moving in prophetic ministry at this time and personal prophecy. I began to learn from others and the Holy Spirit how to do it. I became really good at it and my friends would test me and ask me what I see for someone they knew that I didn't know. I would see accurately what they did for a living and what they look like. I was asked what is wrong with someone and I would see a problem in a little boy's mouth which the mom said was accurate. Another friend asked me if there was anything different about some girl he knew and I said I saw her limping. He asked which leg and I said the left and he said yes, she broke her leg and it was her left leg. There were all kinds of people testing me like that.

Later I would go on to do prophetic ministry for people who came to the front of the church for ministry, and I would accurately tell them things about their life that I couldn't possibly know and also share God's heart for them with them. I was very good at that and at one-point others declared that I was a prophet. Now let me explain something before you jump to conclusions. You may be thinking mental issues and a prophet? Sure… but prophetic ministry isn't all that mystical or crazy. You don't actually hear voices or hallucinate. I saw pictures in my mind about people or movies in my mind that had to do with them. I would hear a phrase or word in my mind that would come to mind or I would get a divine knowing or feeling. It's not really crazy at all if you think about it. Who hasn't had something come to mind or saw a picture in their mind? The prophet just empties themselves so that the things that come to mind are about other people or from God and not their own thoughts. My old doctor Dr. Friend also believed I could do accurate prophetic ministry and was behind me in this. He tested me on a couple of occasions and learned there was something to this. It was not uncommon for him to ask me what I saw for someone who he knew that I didn't know. It was great validation to have a psychiatrist believe I was a prophetic minister and could do prophetic ministry.

After a while my wife started to change as I did, at least I thought so. The change was taking years but it seemed like it was there. She would have her bad days and I would have mine. But little by little it was working. I remember others didn't always see it that way, and there were times when we didn't either. I remember when we quit the Church we were attending for a short while to attend another Church that was much closer to home. We justified it with the logic that we would save a lot of gas money. To make a long story short, it was a Church filled with bitter memories.

This Church was filled with "refugees" from our old Church, where our Pastor Tom became sick and the Church eventually split. These people knew our situation and our marriage history. When I asked the pastor at this Church for spiritual advice on dealing with my emotional baggage, he refused. It seemed as though my history made him feel uneasy, as he would change the subject whenever it was mentioned.

The new pastor heard that Darcy and I weren't getting along one day and called me into his office. He proceeded to rebuke me and condemn me for not having a perfect marriage. He told me that the Lord no longer hears my prayers because we have been having marriage problems. He said all kinds of other crazy stuff, and he also accused me of physically assaulting my wife. I am not sure where he got that idea. He even threatened to, "Choke me like that guy he choked last week if he found out that I ever hit her." I was thinking, say what? You choked a guy last week? This pastor clearly had some issues. Once again, I tried to explain our marriage history to him. I hoped he would understand, but he didn't. He actually went so far as to say that we could not be members of his Church because we had marriage problems. This really hurt me.

I felt like the new pastor was telling me that I wasn't a Christian. I had done my best. I was as close to God as I thought was possible on earth, and I was doing what I thought Christ would do. Yet it wasn't good enough for this man. His Church was full of people who were divorced and had marriage problems, and there were Church members who were committing adultery with very little discretion. It was hard to deal with. At one point I remember going to see an astrologer with a friend of mine who my friend knew. I had told my pastor about it and he publicly accused me of having demons for seeing the astrologer. After a verbal altercation, I left that church for good. About 9 years later that pastor died of Parkinson's disease. He had a rather crazy obituary in the newspaper about him being a former gang leader in Chicago who used to beat people over the head and rob them as well as lying about his age to the army and being thrown out.

The Christian beliefs dictated your life in this church and in Christianity as a whole and if you were doing something they didn't approve of they would not talk to you, treat you like an outsider and in some cases kick you out of the church. They had scriptures talking about how a person in sin or something Christianity doesn't approve of is to be cast out and turned over to satan. They at one time told me of a couple that was coming to church who lived across the street from the church building. They said the couple was living together and were no married, so they told them that they are living in sin and banned them from coming to church. They said they handed them over to the devil. This is yet another red flag of a cult. And it wasn't just confined to this church but was happening all over in Christianity. Like I said it was even in their bible.

My experience was also an example that is found all throughout Christianity of how they scared people with the fear that if they do something that Christianity doesn't see as Godly then demons would possess them. This is also a red flag of a cult that didn't sit well with me, but I still loved my faith and couldn't see the writing on the wall.

* * *

We ended up leaving that church and going back to Pastor Greg's Church. We decided that the cost of gas was worth the price of belonging to a Church filled with love and acceptance rather than judgment and condemnation. Or so we thought it was full of love and acceptance, but we found we were never good enough for these people as well.

Something else I began to see in Christianity was they were interested in power, power in our nation's politics and laws, power in the community and power in people's lives. This is a mark of a cult for sure, but they don't see it that way they see it as God's kingdom manifesting on earth. They see this as a righteous thing.

* * *

Darcy continued to change as the years went by. She stopped swearing and threatening people at least in front of me, and she became increasingly more loving and kind. She stopped flying off the handle at every little thing, and she began developing manners and social skills. She also began treating me much better, and I was obliged to reciprocate. And the children were turning out to be great kids. I fell in love with the twins from the first moment I saw them, and I loved them as my own. We ended up having a DNA test on the twins, and it confirmed what we already knew. They weren't mine biologically, but it didn't matter.

So, we returned to Pastor Greg's Church. I ended up going through a degree program at a traditional well-known Bible College, and I completed my pastoral internship with Greg as my mentor. I liked this Bible College much better than the correspondence school I had taken earlier. The education I received at the traditional Bible College was great or so I thought at the time, and I bought it all hook line and sinker. The Bible college would help me later in my career when I became the pastor of a few churches. It was a challenge, and I loved it.

One thing I noticed though about Christianity was they hung on every word of scripture and had an extreme fixation on the Bible, it was if the Bible was God and they worshiped it. If something didn't line up word for word with scripture, they thought it to be evil. I couldn't figure out how that made sense? How could we rely word for word on what people thought to be inspired by God but was done with human hands as if it was God himself speaking? How could a book be more important than God? Aren't humans prone to error? Another mark of a cult for sure.

While I was graduating from Bible College I actually got hired as a rural mail carrier for the United States Postal Service. I had tried to get hired there for years but it wasn't happening. Back then in order to get hired you had to pass the postal exam and get the highest score on it, or you wouldn't get an interview, and then if they selected you from the people, they interviewed you got hired. Well, I scored high and got hired. I was so proud and was very good at my job. I ended up working there for several years.

Around this time, I also started a prophetic ministry online. I would do personal prophecy, write articles, and books and do dream interpretation for donations. It worked out great and we got regular traffic and requests on a daily basis. A couple of other popular Christian prophetic sites also published my articles. A friend financed my prophetic online ministry and believed in my doing prophetic ministry. He financed a lot of other things for me as well, including the traditional Bible College which was expensive. He also thought all the spiritual experiences I was having were interesting. He became my mentor and taught me the ways of the world and about people. I learned a great deal from that man and appreciated all his help. He was like a father to me. He was not an evangelical Christian, and he is what I come to find a kinder person than anyone I ever met in a church.

Over time I began to change, and I actually studied people and how things worked. I wanted to know why they do what they do and why they think the way they think. I was certainly becoming wiser than I had previously been. I now had goals and rarely got angry and could focus. I was accomplishing, I was pretty happy and things were going well.

Then not long after that I got ordained for the first time and was put into my first church to pastor but it didn't work out too well. The Church had lost almost all its congregation, and no one was really left. So, I left that Church, and I started a Church in my town. The new Church didn't get very big, but I did get a small congregation and it went okay for a while until we decided to move out of the area then I closed it down.

Darcy and I also had another child, and we named her Lizzy. We moved to a newly built house in the country with river frontage and acreage, all in a beautiful valley setting. In a new area. We tried attending a church in that area but it didn't go well. My wife didn't like that church because the drums were too loud. I wanted to give it a try though so I thought to ask the pastor if there was a way to turn down the drums as my wife was concerned about our baby's ears. He became enraged and said who do think is more important God or your baby's ears! After that he was out to get me. We ended up having problems there and left. I learned that in Christianity If something humanitarian came in conflict with their Christian practice, they would be against it and have a hard heart towards it. This made no sense to me and made these people seem really bad but again it's a mark of a cult.

* * *

So I started another Church in a small nearby town (actually the town I grew up in) and that grew quickly. We got a congregation and a building of our own. I started a thrift store and that seemed to make enough money to pay the bills and it helped people as we often gave stuff and money away and had a food pantry. Then after a little while I ran into a snag with the city over our building code, so I decided to turn the thrift store over to someone else, close the Church, and take a job as a pastor of another Church 30 miles away. This was a very old denominational Church. It was actually a congregational Church, and it didn't go so well. But I started another thrift store in a nearby town.

As time went on, I thought we had it pretty good, life was good. Until one day I walked into our thrift store that we owned. Darcy was working there during the day running it. I was on my way past there headed somewhere and I decided to stop there and see my 3-year-old daughter who went to work with Darcy that day. So I stopped and my daughter was sitting alone in the back room. I asked her where her mother was and she said, "In the bathroom with Shay." Shay was the town cop who seemed to be stopping into the store a lot to chat with Darcy. I warned Darcy about spending time with him because I had heard that he always came in there and that Darcy would flirt with him. I warned her that if you flirt with him that things can lead down a road to adultery again. She said that she wasn't doing anything wrong and our conversation ended.

As I talked to my daughter I saw Darcy come out of the bathroom putting her shirt on. She came out alone, but he was still in the bathroom. They must have heard me talking to Lizzy. When she came out she said, "Hi," and I said, "I know what's going on," and I left. She was cheating again. How could she repeat the past after all that we went through trying to fix the marriage? I was beside myself with hurt. Later on, that day when I got home and she was home, I talked with her and she admitted having sexual relations with him and that there was nothing wrong with it. She also admitted that it happened many times and that it was an affair. I later found out that Darcy had not changed all that much. People told me she would still swear and threaten people and act terribly when I wasn't around. She just watched her act around me. The change I thought I saw was not real, it was fake, just a show for my benefit. She was not repentant and thought nothing was wrong with her actions and having the affair, it was clear she was going to keep it up.

In the end, we divorced and went our separate ways. It just didn't work out even though we tried and gave things more of a chance. It had reached an end. Although before the divorce was final, I asked her if we could work it out and get back together and she said no. She said she had a new boyfriend who she loved and that she would not go back to me. That was that the marriage was over and the divorce was later finalized. The rest was pretty hard, divorce stinks and it hurts. It feels like your best friend died. The cop later lost his job as he was on duty when he did this and I turned him in. That was a battle trying to go up against a cop but he did wrong. The man knew she was married and was a pastor's wife but didn't seem to care. Healing from divorce is a whole different story but you do heal with time I did my best to make the most of the marriage. I made some mistakes and I could have done things differently, but it is what it is. I maybe could have tried again to make it work if she was willing but she wasn't.

Chapter 5

Life After Divorce

After the divorce life got really hard, bad stuff happened. I wasn't a pastor anymore or preaching anywhere and my life was changing. Just before I caught my ex-wife with the cop I had gotten a position as an associate pastor of a local Baptist church. But when they heard I was divorcing they demanded that I resign, and they basically told me I can never do ministry again. No longer did I have a spouse. I learned to live as a single parent. I also closed the thrift store. Right away I turned the cop in for having sexual relations with my wife while he was on duty. It is hard to explain how you do that because he was also the chief of police, but I figured it out and the county police and the town investigated him. All kinds of things came out that he was doing, and he was even charged with a felony. I really became consumed to see that he is no longer a police officer. Really, I should have just turned the other cheek, but I didn't. Within the following year he went to jail for a week and was convicted of a felony. He resigned as a police officer and became a milk delivery man.

My ex-wife moved out after the divorce, and she really went wild. I got the placement of the 3 boys which included the twins, and she had our daughter. Then in the summer, she would have them all for a couple of months. That didn't work out too well and she actually shacked up with sex offenders and got into drugs and alcohol really badly. All her boyfriends were always sex offenders and criminals and she was always up to no good. She could not remain faithful to anyone and was often cheating on a current boyfriend with three other guys. After a year I would also get our daughter full time and would be raising all four of my children.

I went on with my life though.

As time went on all kinds of bad stuff happened to me. My mental issues came back and I had to go back on meds and because of that, I gained 70 pounds. I had to have one of my kidneys removed because they found a non-cancerous tumor on it and told me it was cancer until they removed the kidney and tested it. My back went out for a couple of years and I tore my Achilles tendon in half. I was not having a happy divorce. The mental illness got really bad. I was having terrible anxiety and panic attacks. I couldn't go anywhere or leave the house. I also couldn't concentrate on anything. Then depression set in. For years I had no energy, and I could not do simple things. I could barely cook a meal. I lost interest in everything and could do nothing. It was even hard to lift my arm to change the channel with the TV remote. I know that sounds strange and maybe even unbelievable, but it was true. I had no energy to do anything. Everything was extremely hard, the anxiety was the worst, and I couldn't sit still either. I would even get woken up at night not being able to breathe from panic attacks. If my mood was not down, it would go too high up and I would have some highs.

I did, however, get my daughter full-time as well as kept my other kids. To date, things have gotten way better.

I had done some ministry for a while since the divorce (although being divorced most churches and Christians judged me and said I can never do ministry again), my mental health issues got better, and I had a stable mood. Been able to accomplish a lot of things lately. I became a local firefighter, got a real estate license, did a hobby farm, lost 70 pounds, am thin and in shape again, and so much more. I found much peace and happiness but have realized a lot of things. Christianity was not what it was supposed to be. God didn't fix my wife; he didn't hold my family together and he didn't really heal me. The people in the churches I attended turned out to be some really awful delusional people and despite the preachers promising if you tithe and give ten percent or more that God would make you rich, I was not.

Chapter 6

The Truth

Over the years I have come to realize that much of Evangelical Christianity was a lie. When I walked into the Christian world so many years ago, I became immersed in a world that was both amazing and frustrating all at the same time. Amazing because God made Himself real to me but frustrating because evangelicalism never seemed to work for me.

Then there were the Trump years and election mixed with COVID that made me rethink Christianity quite a bit. That seemed to bring out the worst in Evangelicals. Any idiot could see that Donald Trump was not Christ-like and had issues. Anyone should have been able to see that we should walk in love towards people and care for the poor. There was so much hate coming out of the Trump camp, so many delusions and things that just downright make a person sick. I will tell you right now I am not a democrat, and I will admit they don't have all the answers either, but the Trump Republican party was some messed up stuff. I was attending a church at the time Trump was running for re-election and one of the pastors (after Trump lost) was actually telling people that there needs to be a rebellion and people need to die. He was calling for murder! Crazy stuff! There were so many other crazy things that I saw that I will not get into that had to do with Trump and COVID, but I think you get the point. There was a lot of nonsense going on and Evangelicals were right at the heart of it.

I have found that God is good, Evangelicalism is bad! Keep God, throw out all the theology, the literal interpretation of the Bible and church bullshit, and you may have something.

Chapter 7

Church Mayhem

I attended the Assembly of God church in Wisconsin during the whole year of 2020 and the first part of 2021. What I saw and heard was shocking and leaves me very grieved. As you know the pandemic began in 2020. And throughout the whole year all 4 of the pastors (Marcy, Dave, Roddie and Arnie) of this church stood up many times and said that COVID was a hoax and that masks were evil. They told members of the church to refuse to wear them when they go into businesses even though businesses were requiring them and it was state law, to not wear them in church. They said that God told them personally that Donald Trump was going to win re-election and that anyone who didn't vote for Trump was going to hell. They stressed that Trump was a godly man chosen by God

Then when vaccines were coming out, they told everyone not to get one and that the vaccine was the mark of the beast and you would go to hell for getting it. They added to that and said vaccines contained microchips and aborted baby parts. Pastor Arnie said that more than once from the pulpit. COVID went through this church and 4 or 5 people were hospitalized in critical care and one died. They shrugged it off and said COVID did not come from their church and it is not their fault that someone died. I even got COVID from this church myself, it went all over the church and most people got it. The woman who died from COVID had a husband who also attended the church and the pastors of the church kept saying they are so happy that her husband is not sad and that he is acting as a Christian should and that he is a Godly example. It was as if they would have judged him for grieving as he should have grieved. They also told me when I became a member that they don't help the poor and the poor need to help themselves. They said that public assistance was bad and that there was a woman who recently was going there who was on disability for being mentally ill and they kicked her out of the church for not working. They also said she had some other sin in her life. She was very hurt and tried to come back there and they called the police on her.

A person called on the phone at one point to ask for a voucher for a hotel because they were homeless and the pastors (Dave and Marcy) laughed and said they don't help homeless people. I left the church but I remember back in January of 2021 even one of the pastors (Pastor Arnie) was saying that there needs to be martial law and some people may get shot but that Trump and his supporters need to get guns and overthrow the country and even shoot and kill people. I thought that was a shocking statement. He was actually advocating for killing people over the election. I feel like crying just thinking about it I am so grieved. So many crazy things came out of that church. These things were very concerning, and I am upset that a woman actually died from COVID because of this church's policies then they didn't even want her husband to grieve. Very disturbing stuff. Sadly, this is how a lot of evangelical churches and Christians acted. I think the whole virus thing was really blown out of proportion in the world and all but the way some evangelicals acted was shameful.

Evangelical Christianity Is A Cult

Chapter 8

Delusions

There are so many delusions in Christianity from money, miracles, and politics to healing. One thing is for sure not everyone in Christianity is playing with a full deck.

Many ministers get sick and die. John Paul Jackson recently died a few years back of cancer and he was a so-called famous prophet among charismatic evangelicals and I think healing was one of the last courses he taught on. So many other great men and women of faith have gotten sick and were not healed. We can't always say that people are all healed because that is not reality, yet that is what so many Christians believe. We also can't go around saying those that aren't healed lack faith or are in sin because that's not true.

I had a friend who was a preacher for a little while that always preached that God heals everyone and that everyone is always healed. After knowing him for many years, one day I noticed something was wrong with one of his eyes. So, I asked him, "What is wrong with your eye? It looks funny." He said he is blind in one eye and has been since birth. I was shocked. This is the guy who claims that God heals everyone and if you aren't healed you are in sin or lack faith. But I guess what he was preaching was true for everyone else but him.

Another healing revivalist I know had a healing faith course. In the video course he had a pastor teaching who said healing is guaranteed in the atonement and all are healed and if they aren't they lack faith or are in some kind of sin. He showed a picture of the walls of his church, and he had the wall lined from top to bottom with wheelchairs, crutches, walkers and canes. He said those are from all the people he healed in his church over the years. Not long after his teaching video came out, he was diagnosed with cancer and died. He was not healed. The healing evangelist who made the course didn't take him off of there or changed anything. It was hard to believe and leaves you wondering how stupid these people can be.

Then there is the whole blessing thing.

Christians tend to believe that blessings and all good things always come from God and mean they are doing all the right things. They think it means they are pleasing God more than other people are.

Blessings are a wonderful thing. We all want blessings and sometimes we get them, some people more than others. To many they are a stamp of approval by God that they are pleasing Him and doing all the right things. But are they always an indicator of pleasing the Lord? Blessings in the Bible at least in the Old Testament meant that you were obedient and was committed to the Lord. Abraham was blessed and the Bible says his faith and obedience was accredited to him as righteousness (Rom 4:3). His righteousness brought blessings. It says in Gen 13:2, "Abram had become very wealthy in livestock and in silver and gold."

There is also a psalm that speaks that if you are obedient, you always prosper.

Psalm 1:1-3 says, "Blessed is the man who walks not in the counsel of the wicked, nor stands in the way of sinners, nor sits in the seat of scoffers; but his delight is in the law of the Lord, and on his law he meditates day and night. He is like a tree planted by streams of water that yields its fruit in its season, and its leaf does not wither. In all that he does, he prospers."

There are many others in the Bible who were blessed for being obedient and many scriptures that refer to that. For a long time, I thought that blessings meant you were doing something right. For a time, I was really blessed, and I used to brag about my blessings and people used to say I must be pleasing God. Then when bad things happened, I thought I must be displeasing God. I spent a lot of time trying to figure out what I was doing wrong.

I lived that way for a long time, and I have seen so many others that do also. But then I kept seeing another reality. I was seeing some really bad people always get blessed and be successful. And I am talking about some awful people, the kind that molests little children and spread hate and lies toward God and others. The kind that Dr. Phil says should be under the jail! After seeing these kind of things for years you start to realize just because someone has been blessed and good things happen to them or not happen to them does not mean they are doing anything right or wrong. Things just happen.

As the Bible says in Mat 5:45, "That you may be children of your Father in heaven. He causes his sun to rise on the evil and the good, and sends rain on the righteous and the unrighteous."

Too many Christians are taught and think their blessings mean they are something special and too many think their misfortunes mean they are doing something wrong. Even in sermons Preachers often talk of their own blessings as rewards for obedience and faith. It is hard not to think that way, but it is not reality nor is it totally scriptural. It seems that most of the blessings for following the law in the Old Testament were primarily for Israel. And we don't see as much of that in the New Testament or in the things that Christ said.

Jesus talked about misfortunes happening to people and said in Luke 13:4, "Or those eighteen who died when the tower in Siloam fell on them—do you think they were more guilty than all the others living in Jerusalem?"

This terrible event didn't come upon those people because of sin or displeasing God. It is just something that happened. The truth is Jesus wasn't that blessed with good things happening to him or material wealth, he had nothing and was basically homeless, yet he was doing everything right. The disciples pleased God, yet they had such great misfortunes that some of them were tortured, jailed, and martyred. Blessings and bad things are just part of life, they just happen and often it is not because we are doing anything right or wrong. But I guess whether or not you see that is how you interpret the Bible. Not saying the Bible is true or a good book to be putting your faith in, just you could get a couple different interpretations from it on the subject of blessings. Of course Christians usually lean towards the bad one that justifies them and makes them seem special.

I learned not to judge my life or others by the good or bad that happens. Good things will come, and they will go, we can't control what happens no matter what we do. Instead judge a life by the amount of love they put out in the world. If you do that you will never go wrong and will always be blessed. This belief by Christians about blessings is harmful and delusional. For most people the blessings would have come no matter how good or bad the person was. God had nothing to do with it.

Something else Christians have gravitated to is positive thinking, manifesting, law of attraction and name it and claim it. These things are clearly not based in reality and can be harmful.

It is good when people are happy and positive, we are more drawn to people who are. And why wouldn't we want to be? Often times other people's moods and attitudes can rub off on us and shape ours. But we are not in heaven yet, this world isn't perfect. People aren't perfect and stuff happens to people that is downright crap. It can cause people to be sad or worse negative. There has been a movement in Christianity to be positive, some have abused it and used it to try and manifest and attract all kinds of good things to their life. While it helps to be positive it isn't a magic potion. We can't always get what we want by being such. It has caused many Christians to shy away from people who are sad or in a down state of mind. It has caused Christians to label all kinds of things as negative and avoid them like the plague. It even makes some Christian not want to be around people that aren't successful, rich or doing well.

This is not love, love loves even when things are not happy and good. Love loves when someone is down. Love even loves despite the negative.

The Bible says in Romans 12:15, "Rejoice with those who rejoice; mourn with those who mourn."

This is a great passage because it not only says to be excited for people we often get jealous of which is another topic for another time but to also mourn with those who mourn. That is right, be sad with those who are sad. It does not say to avoid them because they are too negative. It doesn't say to throw some Bible verses at them and to tell them to snap out of it. But says to come down to their level and be sad with them. And that is what we need to do is meet them where they are and just have empathy and be human with them.

It is not good to constantly be around negativity but what is love if we can't love those who feel unloved? What is love if we can't love those who hurt and those that have lost hope? Those that have lost happiness and who are depressed.

Christians also tend to do the name it and claim it thing and believe in manifesting positive things into their life which is mainly material things. This is a delusion and does not work, you can't always manifest and draw a mansion into your life just by thinking positively about it coming to you nor can you name it and claim it with Bible verses or just by speaking it as some of them do. This is just not reality and better fit for a mental ward. I think Christians tend to lack in the love department and are too delusional about positive thinking, manifesting and attracting positive things into their lives.

Chapter 9

Evangelical Christianity Is A Cult!

At this point, I can't deny there is a God, but Evangelical Christianity sure seems like a cult!

Some people are shocked by that statement but let's look at the definition of a cult as well as the characteristics of Evangelical Christianity.

The definition of a cult is, "a religion regarded as unorthodox or spurious, a great devotion to a person, idea, object, movement or work (such as film or book.)"

First of all, who sets the bar for what is or isn't orthodox? Because while there are many Evangelical Christians in the world that would argue they are orthodox in belief, there are a ton of people who are not Christians that would certainly categorize Evangelical Christianity as unorthodox. Just because millions of people believe in it does not make it right or orthodox. For thousands of years the majority believed in slavery, and we all know the story of the emperor's new clothes don't we. Many people believing in something does not make it right, does it? Many people are sounding the alarm that Evangelicalism is off these days and people are starting to take notice.

The other part of the definition of a cult that I shared states, "a great devotion to a person, idea, object, movement or work (such as film or book)." Isn't there a strong devotion to religious leaders in Christianity? Don't they seem to fall on every word they say? And don't get me started with Evangelicalism's devotion to a certain political party's political figures. Isn't there a strong devotion to church leadership or the church itself which is make up of persons in which persons are running it? I would say that fits the description of a strong devotion to a person, doesn't it? Is there not also a strong devotion to a Literal interpretation to a book known as the bible? They put the Bible before God Himself. As if God no longer speaks today or is alive. Disregarding the fact that our lives and personal experience with God are actually living scriptures According to the definition of a cult, Evangelical Christianity is starting to measure up.

There is another thing they do that is cult-like, they tend to think that everyone in the world besides them is bad. They like to only associate with other believers unless they are trying to convert you. This is a cult behavior, my friends! They control your life with rules and by their leaders and they also want your money. A minimum of ten percent as a matter of fact. They are delusional, the bible isn't all literal. There is no way the people who wrote it were speaking for God all the time or that some of those things really happened literally. There are contradictions and some of it wasn't originally written till hundreds of years after it happened but passed around orally till then. Do you actually think it is accurate to the very word that was written? Do you really think no one changed anything after it was copied over and over and put in their own ideas and agenda? Do you really think the original writers of it never put in their own ideas and agenda into what they thought God was saying or how they were communicating what happened? Yet Christians take it literally and hang on every word. This is craziness at its finest! They worship the bible and live their life by it. It's like trying to live by Uncle Frank's amazing fish tales in which a bluegill turns into a whale when Uncle Frank didn't mean it to be something literal.

They push church attendance and rituals on you and make you adhere to their standards. They judge and condemn and beat you up with their words. They are hypocritical and don't live up to what they are preaching, yet they expect everyone else too. They push certain political parties and political figures with no regard for logic. They ultimately are threatening punishment and death to those who do not follow their ways. Of course, the death is spiritual, and the punishment is not till after you physically die. But it is the same thing. You are going to die and burn in hell according to them and that scares people! They have strange delusions to defy all logic and common sense, even when faced with evidence.

Evangelicalism is certainly a cult! What else could it be? You can argue that it is a religion all you want, and you are right it is. But the truth is a religion can also be a cult. Evangelical Christianity fits the definition of a cult and sure functions as one.

I am sure we can all find that there is a lot more good in the world than Evangelicalism proclaims. I am sure we will find there is a lot more good in you and a lot more good in me. There is an old quote that says, "If you always look for the bad in people you surely will find it." I am done looking for the bad, let us dig up something positive. I am done with the cult of Evangelical Christianity!

Evangelical Christianity Is A Cult

Chapter 10

So, I Left Evangelicalism

So, 20 years after my born-again experience I finally said quits on Evangelical Christianity. Don't get me wrong, I had the born-again experience and a deep relationship with God. I felt the call to ministry, and I went to a well-known Bible college and got a degree in Biblical studies. Also did an internship under a pastor of my local church. Later I was ordained a few times and actually pastored a couple of very small churches. I even started my own ministry that was prophetic and supernatural. A ministry based on spiritual gifts. I grew as a person and was hopeful for the future. I felt purpose and meaning, at least for a while. I believed everything Christianity told me to believe and I would have died for it. I even felt love and acceptance but that love and acceptance would rarely come from other Christians or the church. The love only came from God and a couple of people in my life that God put there who were not evangelical Christians.

Throughout the years I got a taste of what evangelical Christianity is all about. It seemed to be less about love and walking as Christ walked and more about money, elitism, social cliques, control, manipulation, power, politics, oppression, hate, jealousy, greed, selfishness, pride, lying, delusions, judgment, gossip, slander, criticism and tearing people down. I went from one church to another having terrible experiences with people. And it seemed that the worst of them seemed to be running the church or in the inner circles. I was looking for love, acceptance, and family but that is not what I found.

Now some people will say you just went to the wrong church and my church is not like that. Or maybe the common denominator is you and you are the problem? But I went to their churches also and found the same garbage over and over. I tried my hardest to make this thing work and it just didn't work. It is broken and I don't think it is supposed to work because it is not the genuine article. I have read so many stories and talked to many people who have run into the same problems. Are all these people the problem or is there something wrong with Evangelicalism?

The thing is according to their Bibles you had to be perfect, that's right even though Christ only condemns the religious people for sin and passes judgment on them. The rest of the New Testament goes on and on about having no sin. Sure, there are some parts about grace but if you really read it the majority of it means you have to be pretty perfect. The only people that say you can sin and there is all this grace are the people that openly live in sin or the people that want to get new people into their church. But they still will judge everyone else when it comes right down to it. They just think their crap doesn't stink. That's right they may tell you sin is forgiven, and grace abounds, but they are right there to beat you up when you make a mistake. Is it any wonder why church nut-balls judge so many people? I was talking to a pastor of a church I had attended a couple of years back and he was telling me that they are tearing down the house next to the church that the church owned. I remember the house well it was a nice home. It was all remolded inside and out and it was a place that I would even live in. There was nothing wrong with it so I asked him why they would tear such a nice place down? He went on to tell me that these days everyone lives in sin, and they don't want to rent it out to anyone because they don't want sinners to live there. So, they would rather tear it down. To date, they did end up demolishing it and now they are holier than ever, free of sinners, and delusionally happy.

The truth is most people have to leave Evangelicalism because they will never be accepted or measure up to it. You can't follow and believe the Bible to be literal or Evangelical Christianity if you are a human being. Maybe if you were like they say Christ is, both fully man and fully God you could find the kind of perfection that they are calling for. But as a human, you will never measure up. Then add in all the church's delusions, craziness, manipulation, and control and you really can't be a mentally healthy person and stay in all that.

Lately, I have come to a place where I see that the whole Bible is not literal. I now view it as a philosophical book and not a literal true God-breathed book. I really tried and took it word for word for years. I taught it and preached it from the pulpit. But I see the evidence and it is overwhelming that some of it is made up and changed. I just know that you can't take the Bible word for word as the Evangelical and fundamentalist Christians do. To do so is just not logical. Of course, faith is not a logical thing but there is a difference between faith and just plain old stupidity. So, you have to use wisdom. And wisdom leads you down another road than the literal Bible interpretation.

Then there is the whole moral thing. Evangelical Christians tend to look down on people that are not one of them or that don't go to their church. Many condemn them to hell and say a person is only moral and good because of God. But the truth is I have met many good people who don't fit the mold of a fundamentalist Christian. I recently left evangelicalism, yet I am not planning to go off and live an immoral life. I have met many people who either left Christianity or never were part of it and they live very moral lives and are pretty good people. You don't have to be a Evangelical Christian to be good. I think evangelicals judge too many people and label them as bad when they really aren't. It's tribalism at its worst. Life is hard enough for everybody, we don't need to tear people down too, we need to build up and love them. That's what will make this world a place worth living in.

Fundamentalist Christianity often teaches that there is no good in the world, they say there is no good in anyone. They view everyone besides them and their elite clique as evil. They only see the bad in people. And they live in paranoia about the evil people of the world being out to get them or that their sin will rub off on them. It's no way to live, I lived it for years and am so done with it. There is so much more good in the world than fundamentalism proclaims. So much more good in you and so much more good in me.

Since leaving Evangelicalism I have so much more peace than before. I no longer have to measure up to other Christian's standards and be criticized and torn down all the time. I don't have to go to church and put up with that evil cult or club. I no longer have to fit God into a box of rules in which He can only be or act according to their theology. Last I checked God was all-powerful and the creator of the universe. How can we put Him in Bible jail? For most Evangelical Christians, the Bible is their God. Take away the Bible and they have nothing. They wouldn't know God at all. Yet God existed before the Bible and will exist after it. How sad! Now I have so much peace with God, man, and the world around me. There are no more devils out to get me, no hell waiting to swallow me up, no bad men just waiting to do me wrong or rub their sin on me. I can truly love people. Sure, evangelicals say they love but do they really? How is love part of not valuing anyone? How is love part of criticism, judgment, elitism, money-grubbing, control, manipulation, lies, being jerks, and seeing everyone as your enemy or a child of the devil?

There is peace and life after leaving Fundamentalist Evangelical Christianity while staying I have found there is only death. I wish it could have all turned out different but now I see the truth and the truth has set me free. Free to love, live and learn and maybe find some happiness along the way.

Evangelical Christianity is a cult and can do more harm than good. I have left it and found spirituality outside of it. I have found that there is a God but He isn't like the Evangelical God. The experiences I had in Christianity that were supernatural were real but did not confirm that Christianity was right they only confirmed that there is a higher power and that higher power is good and wants a relationship with us. People have supernatural spiritual experiences in almost every religion in the world. And they aren't Evangelicals. I am convinced that I needed Evangelical Christianity to learn a lot of hard lessons and make me into the person I am today. But I now no longer need it and its role is now finished in my life. I have evolved into greater things. I hope that you too can evolve into greater things and if you are in the Evangelical cult that you see the truth and the truth sets you free.

Contact the Author

and

Please Leave a Review

Thanks for reading my book. I hope you liked it. Please consider leaving a positive review of it on Amazon.com, I would really appreciate it.

If you would like to contact the author, Adam would love to hear from you. Please send him an email at:

elishaserves@hotmail.com

www.ingramcontent.com/pod-product-compliance
Lightning Source LLC
LaVergne TN
LVHW051848080426
835512LV00018B/3145